EARTHTOONS

The First Book of Eco-humor

STAN EALES

WARNER BOOKS

A Time Warner Company

D1227867

This title was originally published in Great Britain by Grub Street.

Warner Books, Inc., 666 Fifth Avenue, New York, NY 10103

A Time Warner Company

Printed in the United States of America
First printing: February 1992
10 9 8 7 6 5 4 3 2 1

Library of Congress Cataloging-in-Publication Data

Eales, Stan.
    Earthtoons : the first book of eco-humor / Stan Eales.
        p.   cm.
    ''Originally published in Great Britain by Grub Street''—T.p.
verso.
    ISBN 0-446-39361-4
    1. Human ecology—Caricatures and cartoons.   2. English wit and
humor, Pictorial.   I. Title.
NC1479.E34A4   1991
741.5'942—dc20   91-36219
                                                               CIP

Cover design by Charles Kreloff

The text of this book was printed on recycled paper.

Dedicated to Mother Earth

"I wish Charlie wasn't so conscientious
about being a lumberjack"

"I don't care what the doctor said,
refined men do not eat unrefined food"

"But hunting never hurt anyone"

"Yeah, I would pay more tax
to have cleaner air"

"Hey hang on — we've already done this one"

"I'm going to put you on a course of antibiotics
— I recommend eating beef three times a day"

"I can hear the roar of traffic"

"I hereby declare open this nuclear fuels processing plant"

I CONSUME, THEREFORE I AM

FALLEN ANGEL (THROUGH THE HOLE IN THE OZONE LAYER)

"If we've been eatin' food containin' preservatives all our lives
then how come we aint well preserved?"

"I am the ghost of environment future"

"Mummy, where do hormones come from?"

"Look – designer pollution"

"Hey you bastard — this false beard is made from real fur"

"They reckon I've got heavy metal poisoning"

Haaoooooooooooooolll...... Haaoooooooooooolll...... Haaoo

"We volunteered to test the world's first biodegradable condom"

I SIMPLY ADORE YOUR RAINFOREST COFFEE TABLE BOOK AND MATCHING RAINFOREST COFFEE TABLE

"I just think that it's been badly art directed"

"What's worse than realizing that we will die someday,
is realizing that we're not terribly alive as it is"

"It says here that he was the inventor
of the internal combustion engine"

"He recycles everything"

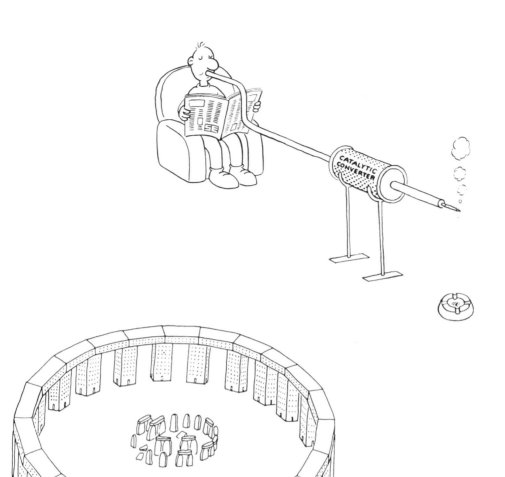

SELF DEFENSE CIRCA 1000 AD

SELF DEFENSE CIRCA 2000 AD

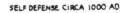

"I used to be a Rodin but I got left out in the acid rain"

"Looks like number 27's lifts are out of order again"

"I just love to hear an environmentalist talking dirty"

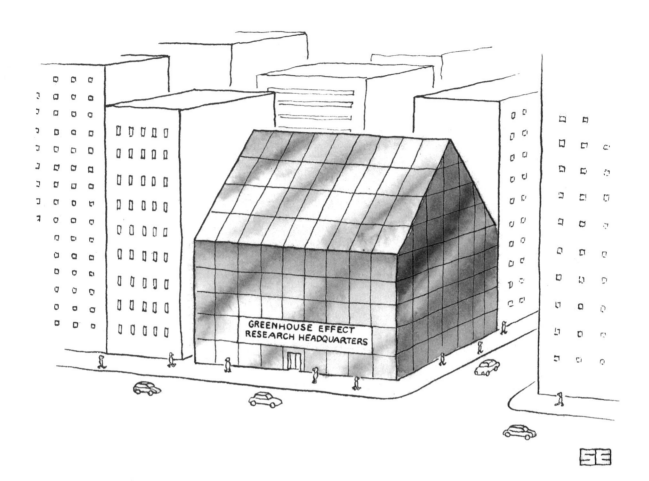

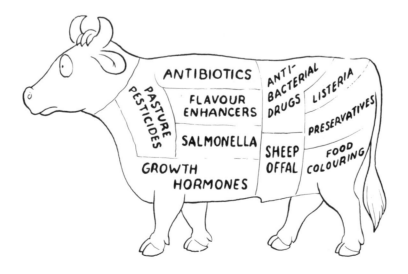

"It must be around here somewhere"

CURB
YOUR
DOG
FINE: $75

RULE OF THUMB FOR FOOD ADDITIVES:

IF YOU CAN'T PRONOUNCE IT, IT'S BAD FOR YOU

MONO DI-ETHOXYQUIN HYDROXYANISOLE

"If this food has no colourings, no flavourings, no preservatives and no added sugar or salt, then why does it cost more?"

"My girlfriend left me for some guy with a catalytic converter"

"The oil slick did wonders for waterproofing the sand"

"Bloody mongrel!"

"One day son, all of this will be hamburgers"

"Trust you to go and stand in some growth hormone"

"If you think they put too much junk in our food,
you should see what they put in their own"

"Lovely sunset this evening"

"You're kidding — this is the stuff they wage wars over?!"

"He appears to have drastically reduced his carbon dioxide emissions"

"Can't be too far from civilization now"

"Hey, he's right — it _is_ easy"

"Sylvia — how could you? You're using cruelty-free cosmetics!"

"We'll be extinct before you're finished!"

"I wouldn't if I were you"

"Hey, it's not an oil slick after all
—it's washed-off suntan lotion"

REBEL WITH TOO MANY CAUSES

"Mind if I smoke?"

"I wonder which is more environment friendly —
to buy a plastic Christmas tree
or to cut down a real one"

"It's acid snow"

"Imagine the amount of advanced technological expertise that went into producing this lot"

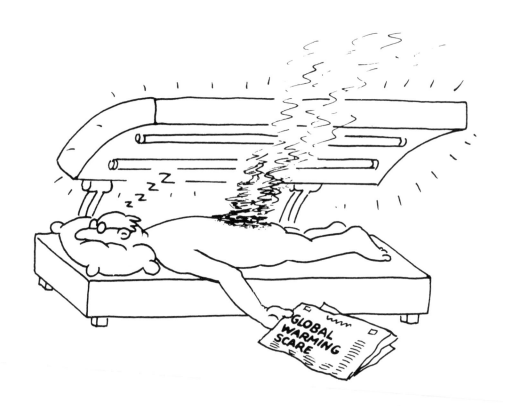

"The neighborhood sure has changed since I was a kid"